THE RAILROAD TERMINOLOGY COLLECTION

The Illustrated Railroad Glossary
Volume 1

101 Common Railroad Terms

Glen R. Landin

CREATIVEARTISTIC PUBLISHING
WWW.CREATIVEARTISTICPUBLISHING.COM
ORANGE, CALIFORNIA

ISBN 978-0-615-87642-9

EBOOK CD-ROM EDITION: AUGUST 2009
PRINTED EDITION: OCTOBER 2013

PRINTED IN THE UNITED STATES OF AMERICA

WWW.GLENLANDIN.COM

GLEN R. LANDIN

ALL ABOARD

[all a·board]   adverb

Refers to the announcement call given by the conductor before leaving a station, or an unscheduled stop on a passenger train

GLEN R. LANDIN

ATTENDANT

[at·ten·dant] **noun**

An employee who assists sleeping car, and coach car passengers with their accommodations and special requests

Baggage Car

[bag·gage car]   noun

A special car which is connected behind the
tender and used to transport luggage and
small freight

GLEN R. LANDIN

Baggage Wagon

[bag·gage wag·on]   noun

A manual four-wheeled luggage cart designed to transport luggage between the platform and the station

Ballast

[bal·last]   noun

Small crushed rock or lava pieces placed in between railroad ties to secure track sections from movement and water damage

BELL

[bell]   noun

**A warning device mounted on the engine
alerting people and animals of an oncoming
train or yard operations**

Boiler

[boil·er]   noun

The cylinder shaped part of a steam engine used to convert water into steam in order for the engine to move and operate

GLEN R. LANDIN

Box Car

[box·car]   noun

**An enclosed railcar designed to transport
many different types of products and goods**

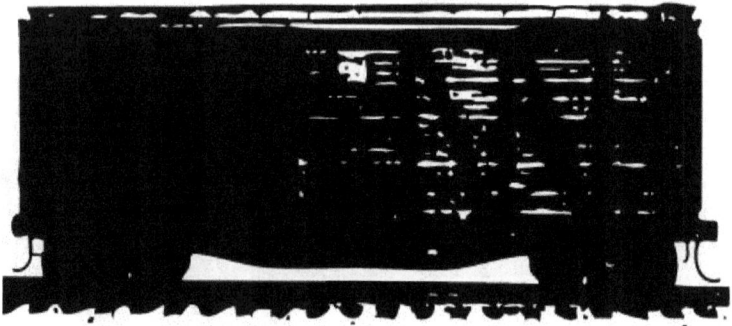

Brakeman

[brake·man]   noun

An employee who assists the engineer with operations on a passenger train or freight train

BUMPER

[bump·er]   noun

**A wooden or steel brace which absorbs shock
and prevents railcar damage at the end of a
track section**

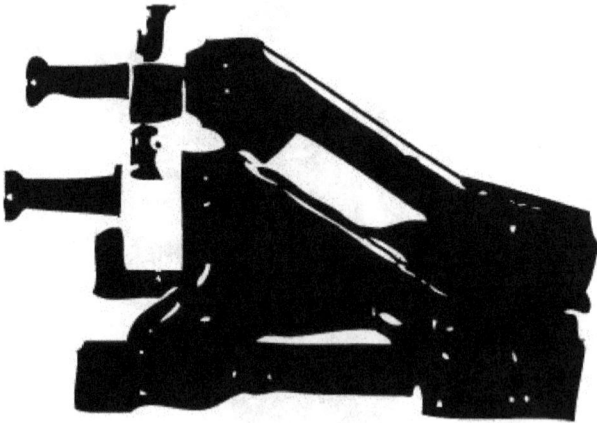

CAB

[cab]   noun

An enclosure located on the engine, which protects operating controls and the crew from the weather

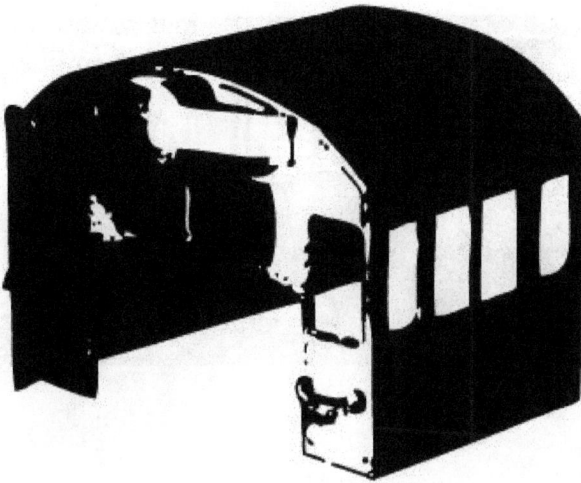

GLEN R. LANDIN

CABLE CAR

[ca·ble car]   noun

A motorized railcar designed to operate in small towns or with limited amount of space

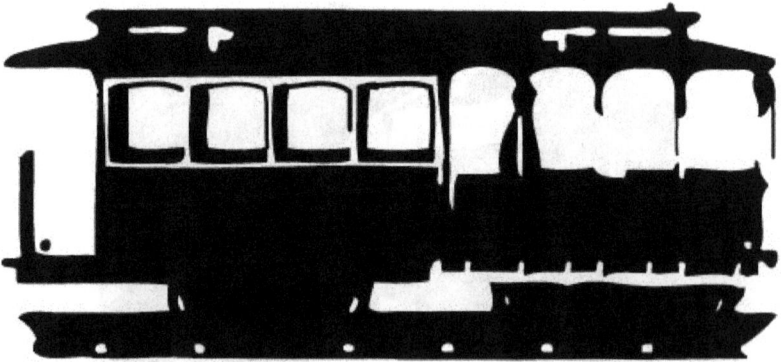

Caboose

[ca·boose]   noun

A special freight car attached to the end of a
train providing an office, small kitchen,
and restroom

COACH CAR

[coach car]   noun

An enclosed passenger car providing restrooms, overhead storage, and seats for transporting passengers

Coaling Station

[coal·ing sta·tion]   noun

A tall structure which coal is stored and used in gondola cars and tenders

GLEN R. LANDIN

COMBINE CAR

[com·bine car]   noun

A divided passenger car which is used for
carrying passengers, luggage, and small freight

COMMUTER TRAIN

[com·mut·er train]   **noun**

A light rail train system designed to transport passengers between suburban areas

CONDUCTOR

[con·duc·tor]   noun

An employee who advises the engineer, collects tickets, and assists passengers en route and on the station platform

Coupler

[cou·pler]   noun

A steel shaped claw or hook located on every railcar and engine which connects all the cars together

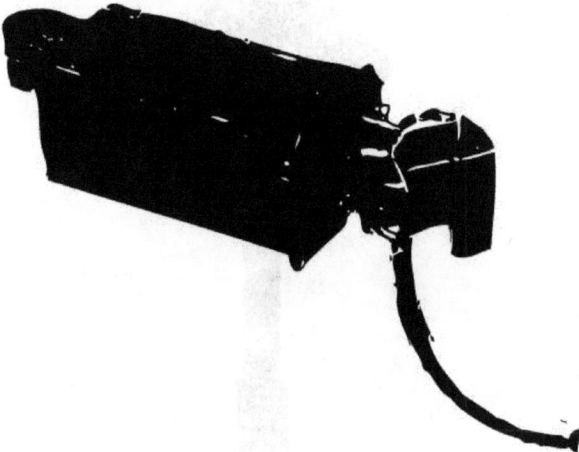

GLEN R. LANDIN

CROSSBUCK

[cross·buck]   noun

**A simple railroad sign located at most crossings
which indicate the presence of railroad tracks**

CROSSING

[cross·ing] noun

A location along a straight or curved track section where streets and railroad tracks meet together

CROSSING GATE

[cross·ing gate]   noun

A long red and white arm extending over the road which prevents vehicles from continuing when trains approach

CROSSING SIGNAL

[cross·ing sig·nal]   noun

A signal consisting of railroad signage, flashing red lights, and bells

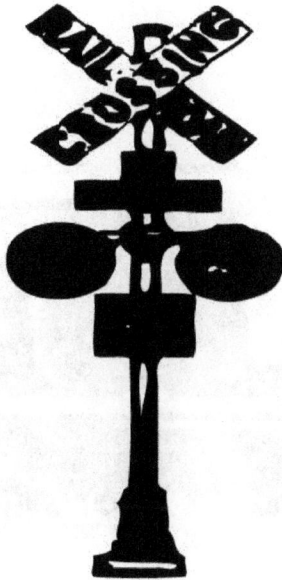

Cupola

[cu·po·la]   noun

**A square box located on top of a caboose
with windows which provides the viewing area
for the brakeman on a freight train**

Depot

[de·pot]   noun

A small railroad building which provides passenger and freight services in small towns and rural areas

GLEN R. LANDIN

DIESEL ENGINE

[die·sel en·gine]   noun

A modern type internal combustion engine
producing additional power which is capable
of pulling heavier and longer train loads

26

DINER CAR

[din·er car]   noun

A special railcar providing passengers with full meal service during their trip

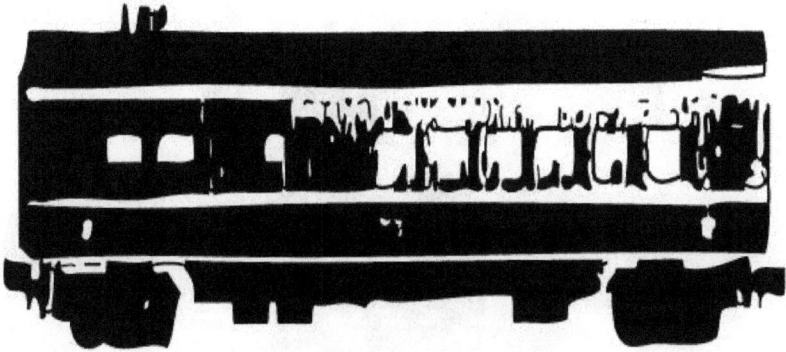

Dispatcher

[dis·patch·er]   noun

An employee who performs train yard, and mainline duties while assisting the engineer and brakeman with moving rail equipment

DOME CAR

[dome car]   noun

**A railcar built with a raised bubble
area on top of the roof which is used for
passenger viewing**

Drawbar

[draw·bar]   noun

A steel part which connects the steam engine and tender securely together

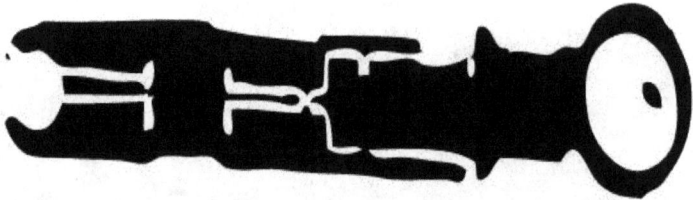

ENGINE STALL

[en·gine stall]   noun

**A small facility with one or two stalls which
are used for locomotive storage and repairs**

GLEN R. LANDIN

Engineer

[en·gi·neer]   noun

**An employee who operates any type of
steam or diesel locomotive**

32

Excursion Car

[ex·cur·sion car]   noun

A lightweight open passenger car designed for optimal viewing on tourist and theme park railroads

Fireman

[fire·man]   noun

An employee who assists the engineer in the
cab of a steam engine, and shovels coal,
watches the firebox, and gages

Flat Car

[flat·car]   noun

A simple freight car which is used to transport heavy and oversized materials

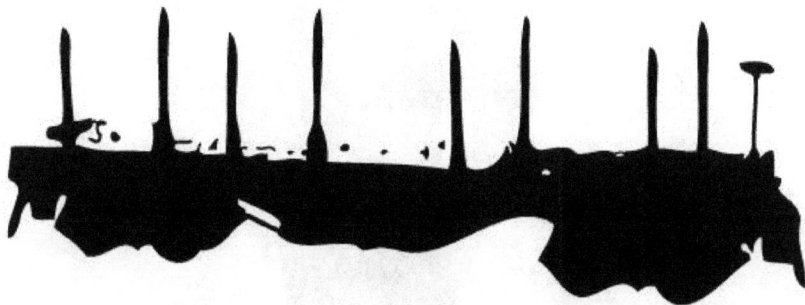

GLEN R. LANDIN

Foreman

[fore·man]   noun

An employee who is in charge of all rail yard workers and operations

FREIGHT CAR

[freight car]   noun

Refers to any type of railcar which is designed to transport many different types of products and materials

GLEN R. LANDIN

FREIGHT STATION

[freight sta·tion]   noun

A small railroad structure which is used for
freight service and storage purposes

FREIGHT TRAIN

[freight train]   noun

A train consisting of freight cars and able to transport oversized, heavy products, and materials

GANDY DANCER

[gan·dy danc·er]   noun

An employee who repairs and maintains the tracks using special tools and equipment

GONDOLA CAR

[gon·do·la car]   noun

A low-sided railcar designed to transport heavy and bulky materials

GLEN R. LANDIN

Handcar

[hand·car]   noun

A small manual pump rail cart which is used during track maintenance and operated by one or two workers

Hobo

[ho·bo]   noun

A person who rides the rails from one place to the next using railcars on a freight train

GLEN R. LANDIN

Hopper Car

[hop·per car]   noun

An open or closed freight car used for transporting bulky items such as rock, grain, or coal

LANTERN

[lan·tern]   noun

A specially designed metal railroad light used by brakemen or hung from railcars for safety purposes

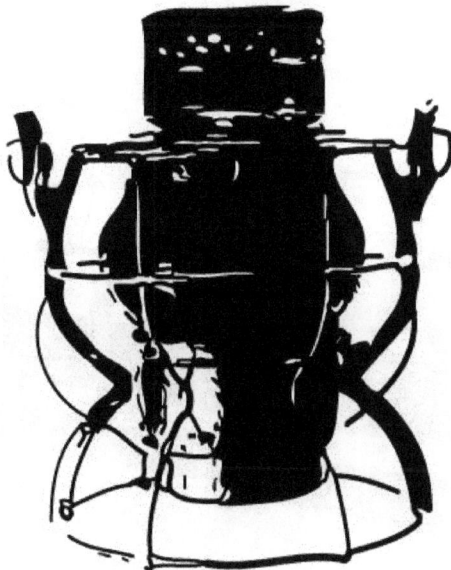

GLEN R. LANDIN

LIGHT RAIL

[light rail]   noun

A modern type rail system with overhead wires which are used for transporting people throughout towns and cities

LOCOMOTIVE

[lo·co·mo·tive]   noun

Any type of self-propelled steam or diesel engine which transports railroad cars

GLEN R. LANDIN

M<small>INE</small> C<small>AR</small>

[mine car]   noun

A small wood or steel type cart which is used for removing rocks and coal from mine shafts

Miner

[min·er] **noun**

A person who searches for precious rocks and minerals within a mine shaft, river, or stream

GLEN R. LANDIN

Motor Car

[mo·tor car]   noun

**A self-propelled motorized rail vehicle used
for track maintenance and safety**

OPERATOR

[op·er·a·tor]   noun

An employee who operates any type of trolley, subway, tramcar, or light rail systems

GLEN R. LANDIN

Ore Car

[ore car]   noun

**A low-sided freight car designed for hauling
bulk ore and coal products**

PASSENGER CAR

[pas·sen·ger car]   noun

A common railcar designed with seating arrangements for carrying passengers to their destinations

GLEN R. LANDIN

PASSENGER TRAIN

[pas·sen·ger train]

A train comprised of passenger rail equipment
and pulled by any type of locomotive

54

Pilot

[pi·lot]   noun

The front end part of a steam or diesel engine which is used for removing large animals, vehicles, or other debris from the tracks

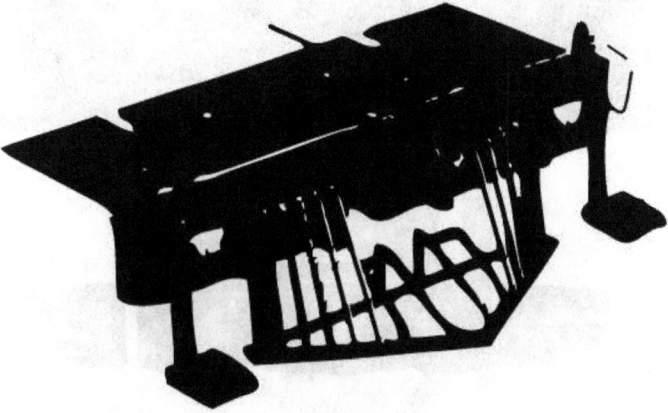

GLEN R. LANDIN

PLATFORM

[plat·form]   noun

**A long covered shelter used for passengers
while waiting for a train**

Porter

[por·ter]　　noun

**An employee who assists sleeping car passengers
with their luggage and accommodations**

GLEN R. LANDIN

PORTER ENGINE

[por·ter en·gine]   noun

A small diesel engine used for short trains
and yard switching of freight cars

PRIVATE CAR

[pri·vate car]   noun

A special passenger car which is elaborately painted and decorated with fine furniture and details

GLEN R. LANDIN

Pullman Car

[pull·man car]   noun

A lavishly designed passenger car which is used for first-class sleeping and coach accommodations

Push Car

[push car]   noun

A small four-wheeled flat rail cart which is used to transport tools and heavy items during track maintenance procedures

RAIL

[rail]　　noun

A long T-section shaped steel which is laid upon crossties to form completed railroad track

Rail Car

[rail·car]   noun

Any four-wheeled type railroad car or self-propelled car designed to transport passengers or freight

RAILROAD PERSONNEL

[rail·road per·son·nel]   noun

A basic term used to describe any type of
train employee or worker

RAILROAD TIE

[rail·road tie]   noun

**A wood, concrete, or recycled plastic tie
length which supports the rails upon a
railroad track section**

GLEN R. LANDIN

Reefer Car

[reef·er car]　　noun

A wood or steel refrigerator type boxcar which transports perishable freight at different temperatures

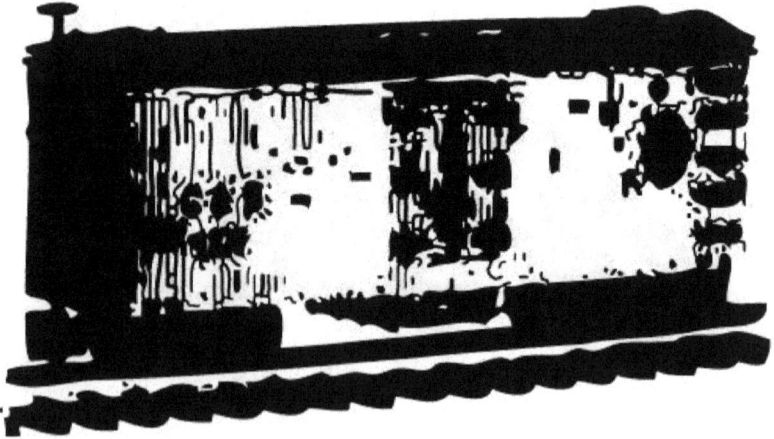

ROTARY SNOWPLOW

[ro·ta·ry snow·plow]   noun

**A large engine equipped with a snowplow
which removes heavy snow from mainline track**

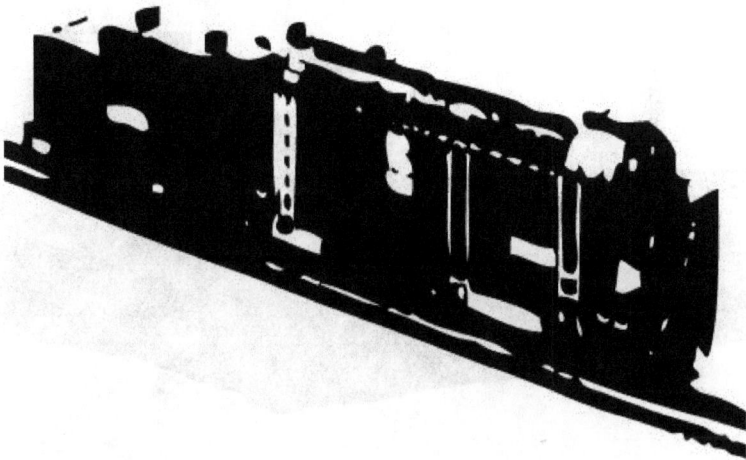

GLEN R. LANDIN

Roundhouse

[round·house]   noun

A large curved building designed for storage and repair of steam locomotives, and rolling stock

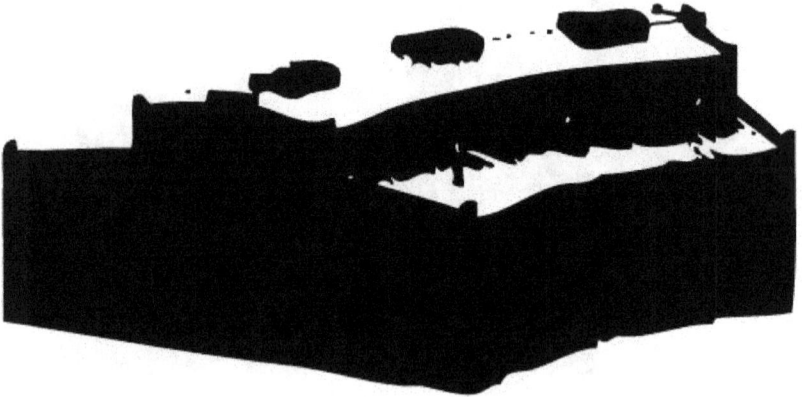

RPO Car

[rpo car]   noun

An abbreviated term for Railway Post Office,
which collates and distributes mail along the
mainline tracks

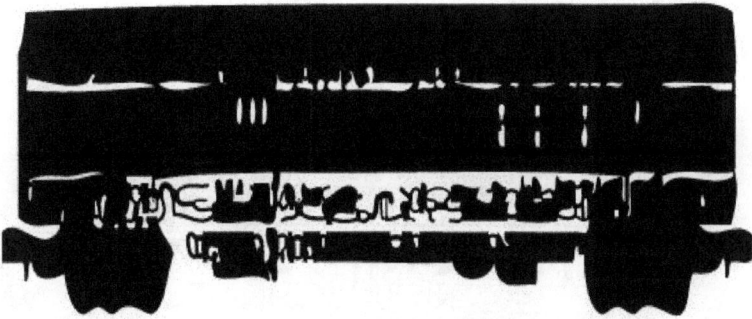

Schedule

[sched·ule]   noun

A printed list of departure and arrival times, cities, and symbols, which is supplied by the railroad

SEMAPHORE

[sem·a·phore]   **noun**

A signaling device with moveable arms and colored lights which controls specific trains along mainline tracks

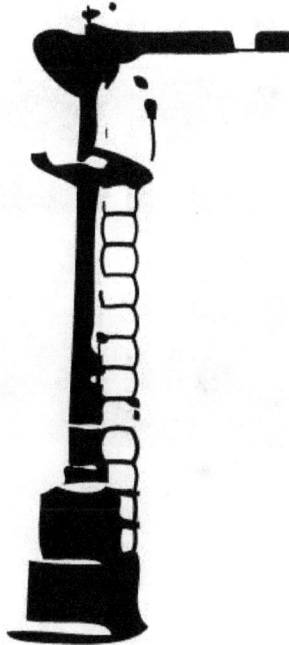

GLEN R. LANDIN

Shanty

[shan·ty]   noun

A small trackside structure which is used for storage and various purposes

SHAY ENGINE

[shay en·gine]   noun

A specific type of logging steam engine designed to operate slowly on steep grades

GLEN R. LANDIN

Signal Tower

[sig·nal tow·er]   noun

A railroad structure used on mainline switching
tracks and controls all passing trains

74

Smokestack

[smoke·stack]   noun

A narrow funnel attached to the boiler of a steam locomotive which emits smoke, cinders, and gases

Spike

[spike]   noun

A large type steel nail used to securely fasten rail onto railroad ties to form completed track

STATION

[sta·tion]   noun

**A railroad structure used for waiting
passengers and or freight services**

GLEN R. LANDIN

STEAM ENGINE

[steam en·gine]   noun

An engine driven and piston system that
produces energy and steam through the
boiler which generates motive power

STOCK CAR

[stock car]   noun

A ventilated freight car designed to transport livestock and other small animals

GLEN R. LANDIN

Streetcar

[street·car]   noun

A self-propelled type railcar with overhead wires and operates through cities and towns carrying people

Subway

[sub·way]   noun

An electric underground railroad which operates on rails under city streets and transports commuters

Switch

[switch]   noun

A moveable rail device which changes the direction of the train either right or left onto a different track

SWITCH STAND

[switch stand]   noun

A manual or automatic device attached to a switch indicating the direction thrown

GLEN R. LANDIN

Telegraph

[tel·e·graph]   noun

A communication system with overhead wires used by railroad companies to contact employees between stations

TENDER

[ten·der]   noun

A self-contained railroad car connected directly behind a steam locomotive which supplies coal and water to the engine

Terminal

[ter·mi·nal]   noun

A large railroad facility which provides passenger, and or freight services, and locomotive maintenance within the train yard

Ticket

[tick·et]   noun

A railroad company issued piece of paper which allows passengers to board the train and indicates their destinations

TICKET AGENT

[tick·et a·gent]   noun

**An employee who assists waiting passengers
with purchasing tickets and train information**

TIMETABLE

[time·ta·ble]   noun

A railroad printed document specifying the scheduled stations, train numbers, times, cities, and passenger accommodations

TRACK

[track]   noun

Refers to any straight or curved completed section of rail, spikes, and ties, which railroad equipment operates onto

TRAINMAN

[train·man]   noun

An employee who works with the train crew and assists the conductor with daily operations

GLEN R. LANDIN

Tramcar

[tram·car]   noun

A self-propelled type railcar with overhead
wires and operates throughout cities and
towns carrying people

TROLLEY

[trol·ley]   noun

A smaller type self-propelled railcar which operates on tighter and narrower streets carrying people

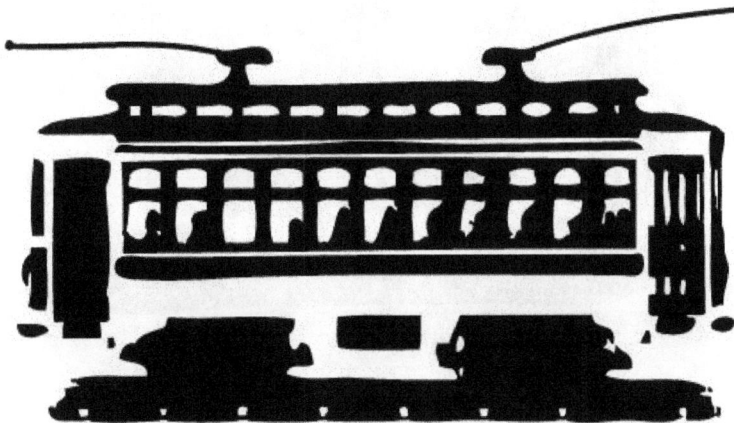

TRUCK

[truck]   noun

**A completed wheel set which is attached
to the railcar underbody**

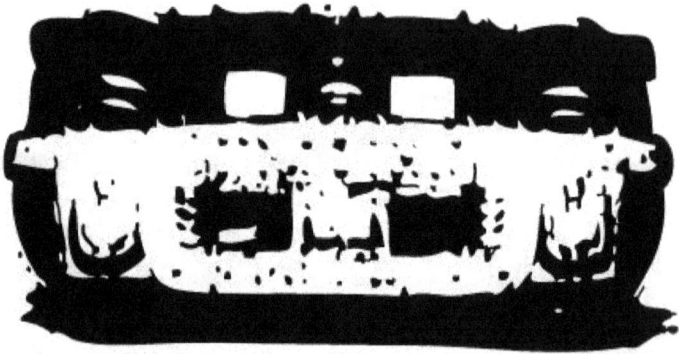

TUNNEL

[tun·nel]   noun

A concrete or wood passageway which trains pass through hills and mountains

GLEN R. LANDIN

Turntable

[turn·ta·ble]   noun

A wood or steel balanced circular rotating platform which moves locomotives and rolling stock onto different tracks

WATER TOWER

[wa·ter tow·er]   noun

A vertical wood or steel reservoir structure which supplies water to steam locomotives

GLEN R. LANDIN

Whistle

[whis·tle]   noun

A device attached to a steam locomotive producing specific high-pitched sounds which alerts employees and other people of railroad operations

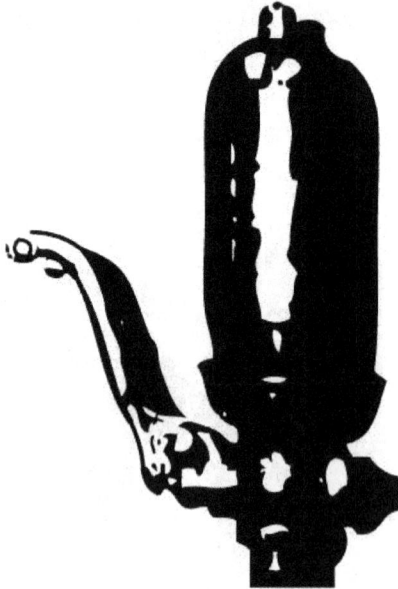

WORK TRAIN

[work train]   noun

A special freight train which performs various mainline track maintenance operations

GLEN R. LANDIN

W<small>YE</small>

[wye]   noun

**A unique Y-shaped track design which reverses
the direction of a train back onto the mainline**

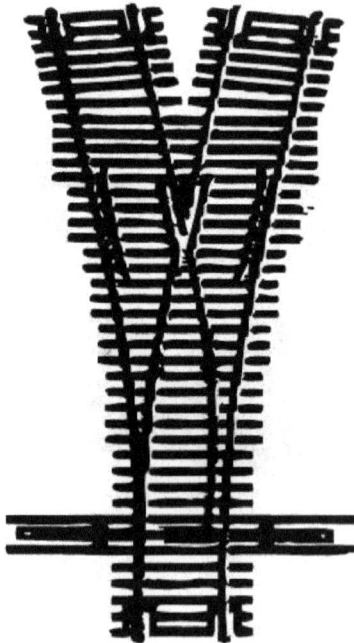

YARD TOWER

[yard tow·er]   noun

A railroad structure located in a train yard which oversees the movement of locomotives and railcars

GLEN R. LANDIN

About The Author

Glen Landin has been sharing his passion of railroading for many years. In The Illustrated railroad Glossary – 101 Common railroad Terms, he combines basic definitions and silhouettes for an interesting visual guide of many train words.

As a creative writer and author, glen also enjoys interior design, photography, model railroading, visual displays, and traveling to nearby and distant shores.

Through Glen's creative writing skills, using poems, phrases, affirmations, and messages, he inspires, encourages, and motivates people to simply believe in yourself. Because all things are possible to those who believe!

www.ingramcontent.com/pod-product-compliance
Lightning Source LLC
Chambersburg PA
CBHW060120050426
42448CB00010B/1969